Bobby Hull
Superstar

BY SCOTT YOUNG

EMC CORPORATION
ST. PAUL, MINNESOTA

Library of Congress Cataloging Publication Data

Young, Scott.
    Bobby Hull, superstar.

    (His Hockey heroes series)
    SUMMARY: A biography of the hockey star whose
skating career began when he received his first pair of
skates when he was not quite four years old.
    1. Hull, Robert Marvin—Juvenile literature. 2. Hockey—
Juvenile literature. [1. Hull, Robert Marvin. 2. Hockey—
Biography] I. Title.
GV848.5.H8Y68 1974   796.9'62'0924 [B] [92] 74-8368
ISBN 0-88436-104-7
ISBN 0-88436-105-5 (pbk.)

Published by EMC Corporation
180 East Sixth Street
St. Paul, Minnesota 55101
Printed in the United States of America
0 9 8 7 6 5 4 3 2

HOCKEY HEROES SERIES

STAN MIKITA/Tough Kid Who Grew Up
GIL PERREAULT/Makes It Happen
FRANK MAHOVLICH/The Big M
BOBBY HULL/Superstar

It was a typical winter day in the little village of Point Anne on Lake Ontario.

A dozen kids were skating on a patch of ice they'd cleared along the shore of the Bay of Quinte. Both boys and girls among them carried hockey sticks and swarmed after the black rubber puck.

Running among them in his overshoes was a sturdy little fair-haired boy in a snowsuit.

Up the hill a big burly man stopped to watch. He was on his way home from work at the nearby cement plant. Some of the girls were his — as well as the little boy with no skates.

In a few minutes he walked on across the snow to his modest house not far away. His wife looked up as he stamped the snow from his feet and came into the kitchen.

"We're going to get Robert some skates for Christmas," he announced.

"Skates?" she said, surprised. "He won't even be four years old until after New Year's!"

But Robert Hull, Senior, had made up his mind. On Christmas morning the sturdy little boy who'd been named after him raced downstairs to the Christmas tree. The skates were there.

Superstar Hull in NHL
playoff action as the
Black Hawks meet the
New York Rangers.

He went straight to the kitchen and pulled them on. Two of his four older sisters helped him with the laces. Supported on either side by his sisters, he slipped and slid down the hill to the ice. There the usual daily hockey game already had started.

As his mother prepared Christmas dinner, she often went to where she could see the patch of ice. His sisters, one on each side, would skate with him and then let him go. He'd try to skate. He'd fall, get up, fall, get up. He was out all day, with only a quick break for lunch.

It was nearly dark at the end of the short winter afternoon when his mother called them all in for Christmas dinner. "By that time," she told people later, "Robert didn't need help from his sisters any more." That's the name the Hull family always call him even yet — Robert.

Soon Bobby Hull's Dad bought him a small hockey stick. He sawed the handle off short. From then on Bobby was on the ice, chasing a puck every second he could manage.

It was common for him to get up before anyone else in the family. He would put the porridge pot on the stove and go out to skate until breakfast was ready. Then he'd eat and go out again. It would be dark some nights when the Hulls would send one of Bobby's sisters out to bring him in for bed.

One evening his father was standing quietly at the side of the ice watching a pickup game. There was a stir of excitement in him. It wasn't just fatherly pride. In a big family — eventually there were eleven Hull children — a father sees the good points as well as the bad points very clearly.

Record-setter, Bobby Hull, scored his 400th goal in this game against the Boston Bruins on January 7, 1968.

But there was no doubt in his mind. Robert was making plays and handling the puck as well as boys twice his age. The thought framed in his father's mind — "He's going to wind up in the National Hockey League some day!"

The nearest city, only a few miles away, was Belleville. Every Saturday morning the Belleville boys played in organized leagues. Bobby's Dad took him to play in the Belleville leagues when he was ten. He was too good for his own age group, so he was put in with fourteen- and fifteen-year-olds.

Black Hawk Bobby Hull throws a check on his Montreal opponent as he fights for the puck.

One day when Bobby was eleven, Scout Bob Wilson of the Chicago Black Hawks came to Belleville to watch a junior game. Junior hockey in Canada is for boys twenty and under, many almost ready to turn professional.

The Chicago scout got to Belleville several hours before the junior game. He went to the rink anyway. He knew there'd be some kind of game going on. Bob Wilson noticed a burly fair-haired boy; not tall, but obviously strong. Nobody could get the puck away from him. Whack! It was in the goal!

"What's that kid's name?" he asked another bystander.

"Bobby Hull," he was told. "Some kid! There are days around here when he starts with the bantams, then gets into a midget game if he can. If somebody doesn't show up for a juvenile team he gets in there too. I've seen Saturday mornings when I'll bet he's scored twenty goals in four different leagues!"

Bob Wilson had seen and heard enough. He went to a pay phone and dictated a telegram to the National Hockey League headquarters in Montreal. He put eleven-year-old Bobby Hull's name on Chicago's negotiation list.

The rules for recruiting young players have been changed since then. Now only players much older can be tied up by a professional team. But in those days it was possible to put a boy of any age on a negotiation list. That meant no other NHL team had the right to his services.

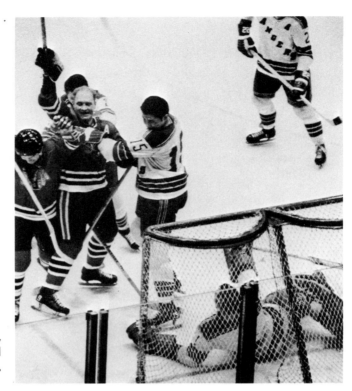

An excited Bobby Hull, after scoring his 50th goal of the 1969 season.

Bob Wilson found Bobby's father in the rink too. He got Mr. Hull's approval. "But don't let Robert know right away," Mr. Hull told Bob Wilson. "It might give him a big head."

A couple of winters later they did have to let Bobby Hull in on the secret. Bob Wilson had been back often, watching Bobby develop. Now he told Bobby's parents that the boy was ready for better competition, better coaching.

He wanted them to let Bobby play on a Chicago-sponsored juvenile team in the town of Hespeler, nearly 200 miles away. He'd have to live there. Juvenile hockey is for boys seventeen and under. Bobby was thirteen.

Mrs. Hull was against it. She and all her children were very close. Her husband argued the other way. "It's Robert's big chance," he said. "We shouldn't hold him back."

Bob Wilson promised he'd find Bobby a good home to stay in. He would be helped and supervised in his school work. Chicago would pay for his room, board, laundry, and school books — along with giving him five dollars a week spending money. Finally Mrs. Hull gave in.

That winter was hard for both Bobby and his mother; the boy being away from home, the mother missing her oldest son. She wrote to him every day and travelled to Hespeler every weekend, often by bus, to see him. His Dad sometimes went along. Mom would ask about his meals and his school work. Dad would stand at the end of the rink and check his son's hockey.

After pulling the goalie out of the net, Bobby flips one past him for a close shot.

A year later Bob Wilson went to the Hulls again. "Robert is too good for the juveniles at Hespeler," he said. "I'd like to move him up to Junior B at Woodstock."

Junior! Bobby was only fourteen. He'd play against boys as old as twenty. Woodstock won the provincial Junior B championship that year. Bobby Hull was a star on that championship team.

During that year, he met another man who would be important in his future. Bob Wilson was proud of his discovery. One day he was singing Bobby's praises to Rudy Pilous, coach of the St. Catharines TeePees. The TeePees played in the Ontario Hockey Association's Junior A League. It was the best amateur league in Canada then, just one step below the professional. The TeePees were also Chicago's main amateur farm team.

"This kid can't be as good as you say he is!" Pilous said.

Wilson had an idea. "He's playing in Woodstock tonight, and your club isn't playing. I'm going over. Come with me and see for yourself."

They drove to the game. Pilous needled Wilson all the way about being so excited. Pilous was a big witty man who had knocked around a lot in hockey. "You scouts are all the same — ten times a year you claim you've found the greatest prospect since King Kong!" Pilous pooh-poohed.

All Wilson said was, "You'll see!"

Pilous did see. He saw fifteen-year-old Bobby Hull who seemed to own the puck. When he was on the ice nobody could get it away from him. On the drive back to St. Catharines, Wilson did the needling. Pilous sang the praises.

"I can hardly wait until we get him on our club next season," Pilous said enthusiastically.

As soon as hockey season ended, Bobby hurried home. His idea of a good time in summer, even as a boy of eleven or twelve, was to take a small axe his Dad had given him and go cut wood with the men. He loved hard physical work. At fifteen Bobby was already developing the physique that later made him the strongest man in hockey and helped him become the greatest scorer of his time.

Again in 1972, Bobby scored his 50th goal of the season. This time it was against the Detroit Red Wings.

Hull in action as Bobby lets go with his famous slap shot.

But soon summer was over. Bobby moved to St. Catharines. By now, he was a veteran of living away from home. His Mother still visited when she could and she wrote every day. His Dad kept his eye on Bobby's hockey. In a game where Bobby got two goals, his Dad would tell him he should have scored five. Mr. Hull was a hard man to please — but he knew the world was hard to please too.

"A man who does any less that what's in him — his very best — never gets very far," he told his son.

It took Bobby Hull six games as a Junior A player to get his first goal. It happened in Montreal, in a game against the Junior Canadiens. But Bobby scored only eleven goals that first season. He was as big and strong as players three and four years older. But he wasn't as mature.

All these years Bobby had always played center. But the next season, Rudy Pilous decided this was a mistake. A center should always concentrate on getting the puck up to his wingers, making plays so they can swoop in on goal. Centers are basically playmakers. Pilous could see that Bobby Hull had the equipment to be one of the greatest scorers if he had a center shaking him loose with passes.

"Look, kid," he said, "we're going to try you at left wing for awhile."

Bobby liked playing center. It was a prestige position among kids, like being a pitcher in baseball or a quarterback in football. It didn't matter to him that among great stars of the time in other sports, Jimmy Brown hadn't been a quarterback or Mickey Mantle a pitcher.

"I'm going to play center or nothing," he said.

Pilous said, "Get off the ice until you're ready to play hockey my way."

Bobby went home to Point Anne for a few days. But he felt lost away from hockey. He went back and apologized. Pilous accepted the apology and backed off a little himself. He'd rather have a happy Bobby Hull than an unhappy one. He let Bobby go back to playing center. That season Hull scored thirty-three goals.

Then he made one other move that showed he was still young and headstrong. He and a St. Catharines girl fell in love and, over the objections of both sets of parents, were married. He rarely talked of that marriage later, except to say: "We were too young." The marriage ended in divorce and both later remarried. Bobby's first son stayed with his mother.

Taking it easy, Bobby glides
across the ice looking for
some action.

Bobby Hull was still in high school. Besides his
hockey-playing, he played fullback for the school's
football team. One of his teammates then was a
younger kid, also a hockey player, Stan Mikita.

One September day in 1957, Bobby scored two
touchdowns in a school game. After the game was
over, he headed back to his boarding house in St.
Catharines. When he got there he found an urgent
message to call scout Bob Wilson. The Chicago Black
Hawks training camp was in St. Catharines that
autumn. Hull had been training with the big team, part
time.

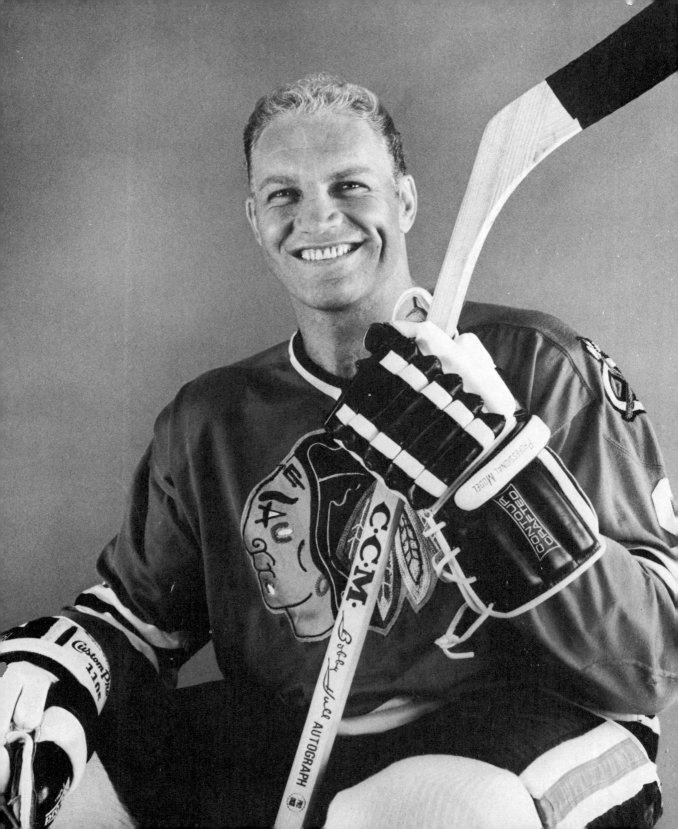

"Get right down to the rink," Wilson said. "I've been trying to find you all afternoon." The Hawks wanted him to play in an exhibition game against the New York Rangers that night!

Bobby was just eighteen, but he had 195 pounds of power in his five-feet, ten inches. That night he played alongside such veteran NHL stars as Ted Lindsay and Tod Sloan, and against some of the best in the game, including the Ranger's Andy Bathgate. But that night Bobby Hull scored two goals.

Tommy Ivan, the Chicago coach and manager, was one of the shrewdest men in hockey. He offered Hull a pro contract.

When the team left for Chicago to start the season early in that October of 1957, Robert Marvin Hull was on the roster. He was then the youngest player in the National Hockey League.

Bobby and some of his co-stars from earlier days, Red Hay, center, and Murray Balfour, left, shave the ice with their flying skates.

1957, Bobby's first year in the NHL for Chicago, saw him taking on such veterans as Boston's goalie Don Simmons and defenseman Larry Hillman.

At that time Chicago had finished last in the National Hockey League, then made up of only six teams, for four years in a row. In the first few months of the season, while Bobby was getting used to the tougher competition, Chicago began to look better.

By the end of that season Hull was recognized as a star in the league. Chicago finished fifth that year. Bobby Hull was on his way. For the next ten years Chicago never finished worse than third.

Hull played that first season as a center, and scored thirteen goals. But a few months after the next season began, Tommy Ivan decided to bring Rudy Pilous in from St. Catharines to handle the coaching.

In training camp the following year, Pilous finally had his way about changing Hull to left wing. It was an historic move. That second season Hull scored eighteen goals. A year later he scored thirty-nine and won the league's scoring championship.

Bobby Hull was only twenty-one. Only one player had ever won the scoring championship at a younger age. That was Busher Jackson of the Toronto Maple Leafs. Jackson had also been twenty-one at the time (1932), but about two weeks younger than Hull was when he won.

The Golden Jet moves in for a shot.

Shutting out his Montreal opponent, Bobby zips ahead to recover the puck from behind the net.

When Bobby looked in the paper after the last game of the season, he couldn't help running down the list of of the men trailing him in the scoring standings. They were the greatest stars of the game.

Bronco Horwath of Boston was second. Jean Beliveau of the Canadiens and Andy Bathgate of New York tied for third. Henri Richard and Gordie Howe tied for the next place, and Boom Boom Geoffrion of the Canadiens was next. But young Bobby Hull was ahead of them all.

The jubilation didn't last long. The biggest prize in the NHL is the Stanley Cup. Montreal had finished first, Chicago third. They met in the first round of the playoffs, in a best-of-seven series.

Montreal won four straight games — and Bobby Hull sat dejected in the dressing room. He'd been hurt. Only played in three of the playoff games. Scored only one goal. Next year, he vowed, it would be different.

It was. Chicago finished third again, and again played the Canadiens in the first round of the Stanley Cup playoffs. Again Montreal won the first game in Montreal. Another rout seemed possible. But then Bobby Hull and his teammates shifted into high gear. They won four games of the next five to eliminate the Canadiens. Meanwhile, Detroit was beating Toronto in the other semi-final.

The stage was set for the Stanley Cup final, the World Series of hockey. There were other stars on the Black Hawks that year, but the big swooping rushes and booming slap shots of Bobby Hull made the difference. The Hawks beat Detroit four games to two and Chicago won its first Stanley Cup in twenty-three years.

From then on, the Hawks were always a team to be feared in the playoffs. Even against stronger teams they were feared, because of Hull and his co-star, Stan Mikita.

But Hull was the workhorse. Sometimes he played regular shifts on two forward lines — meaning double time on the ice. He killed penalties. He was in on the power plays. He was known as the game's greatest scorer.

It wasn't all easy. Hockey is a rough game. Hull has always been a clean player, but clean players get hurt too.

In one playoff series he played with an injured shoulder — frozen so he couldn't feel the pain.

Almost, but not quite. Bobby sprawls on the ice trying to score against Toronto defenders Bruce Gamble (1) and Ron Ellis (8).

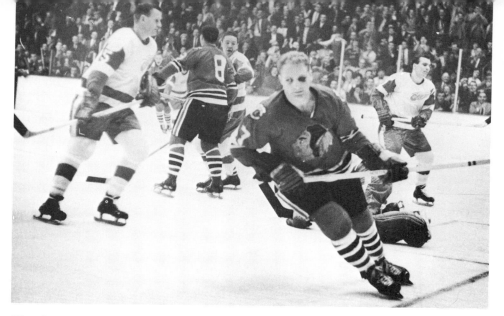

Wearing a colorful black eye gained in earlier action, Chicago's Bobby Hull scores again — this time against Detroit in the 1963 playoffs.

In another his nose was broken and both eyes blackened when he was accidentally hit by a stick. He had to breathe through his mouth, and could hardly see out of one eye. Chicago didn't win that playoff. But Bobby Hull scored eight goals in five games, including three in one game. And he had his nose broken again so that it had to be reset before it had even healed from the first time.

One time he had a stick slammed into his mouth. A sliver of wood was jammed between two teeth. The doctor said he'd have to pull the wood out, then stitch Bobby's mouth. Bobby told him to pull the wood out now, but leave the stitches until later.

"There are only a few minutes left in the game, doc," he pleaded.

His mouth full of blood, he went back to the ice. With the score tied, he shot the winning goal.

25

Another star, Andy Bathgate, said, "You have to stop Bobby in his own end before he gets started — or you don't stop him at all. Once he gets going, he skates over everybody."

That power, and the booming slap shot that was clocked at more than 100 miles an hour, were trademarks of the greatest all-star of his time.

But there was another Hull trademark. Bobby rarely got flustered, on or off the ice. Even after a defeat, when other players angrily brushed past people wanting autographs, Bobby Hull would stop and sign until everybody was looked after.

"If a person thinks enough of me to want my autograph," he said, "I think it's only right for me to stop and talk and sign them."

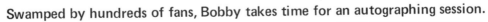
Swamped by hundreds of fans, Bobby takes time for an autographing session.

Looks like this fellow could use some pointers. Bobby shows son, Bart, how to move as Mom looks on.

Also, Bobby was a good Dad. He treasured the time he could spend with his own children. In Chicago he took his sons to practices with him whenever he could. The sight of Bobby Hull on a day off almost always included as many of his children as he could hold by the hand or carry.

Summers were special for the Hulls. Bobby always picked up his family and headed home to Point Anne. As soon as he'd had the money, in the early 1960's, he had bought land and herds of beef cattle. The Hull farms were not far from the Ontario home where he was born. He also built a big summer home on the lake.

Bobby Hull and Brad Park sweep down the ice ready for the next move in an All Star Game.

But even in winter, if Chicago was playing in Detroit, say, and two days later in Toronto, Bobby would take a day off and go to his farm. There on cold February days he would throw bales of hay around as if they were handfuls of feathers. He still loved the hard work.

With all he had done, Bobby still had one special aim. The most elusive record in hockey was the fifty goal record Maurice (Rocket) Richard had scored for the Montreal Canadiens in the 1944-45 season. Gordie Howe got forty-nine one year, but couldn't get the last two. Frank Mahovlich was stopped at forty-eight one springtime. In the spring of 1961, Boom Boom Geoffrion scored his fiftieth, but couldn't break the record. In the spring of 1962, in the last game of the season, Bobby Hull scored his fiftieth, but that was all. The Rocket's record had been tied twice, but not broken.

Then came Hull and the 1965-66 season. Fans were talking again. "Will he break the Rocket's record this time?" they wondered.

At first the chance didn't look good. Hull missed five games with torn knee ligaments. But he recovered and early in March, with three weeks left in the season, he had his fiftieth goal. The fifty-first, for a new record, seemed only a matter of time.

But other teams were checking Bobby ferociously. Each one was determined that if Hull got his fifty-first goal, it wouldn't be against them.

On the night of March 12, 1966, there were 21,000 fans in the Chicago rink. Four thousand of them were standing and all the seats were full. The opposition was the New York Rangers, with Cesare Maniago in goal.

Bobby flips one past Gump Worsley in this 1966 Chicago-Montreal game.

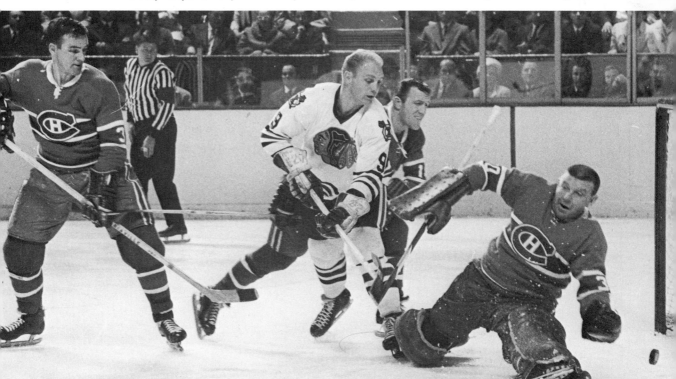

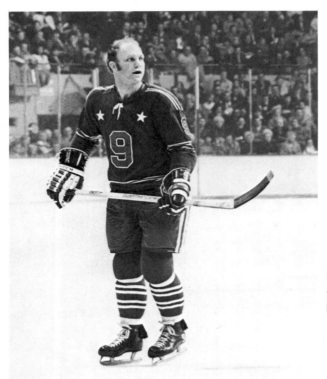

NHL All Star Bobby Hull takes to the ice for the big game.

In the third period, the score was 2-1 for the Rangers. Bobby still hadn't scored his fifty-first goal. Then the Rangers drew a two-minute penalty. They would have to play one man short.

Coach Billy Reay sent Bobby out on the power play. As the Chicago attack formed up, all eyes were on Bobby.

Bill Hay and Lou Angotti passed the puck between them. Then they got it up to Hull. Bobby was skating slowly as he crossed the New York blueline, luring the defenders toward him. He was hoping to let a teammate get in position to take a pass or pick up his rebound if he shot.

Erick Nesterenko dashed toward the goal. Goalie Cesare Maniago was watching closely for signs that the famous Hull slap shot was coming.

Bobby fooled him — by mistake. He said later he didn't get a good shot away. It skimmed along the ice. Maniago moved his big goal stick to stop it. But as the puck arrived, Nesterenko tipped Maniago's stick. The puck went in!

Moving fast, Bobby reaches out to scoop the puck back into control.

As the crowd roared, only Hull was quiet. He stood still. If Nesterenko's stick had touched the puck, it would be Nesterenko's goal.

But the official scorer had seen it all the way. His voice rolled out over the loudspeaker. Goal by Bobby Hull!

Nobody heard anything more. The crowd erupted in a seven-minute standing ovation. Hats were thrown on the ice.

Bobby went over to his wife, Joanne, sitting behind the protective glass in a rail seat.

"Well, I made it," he called to her. She kissed his hand through the glass.

In 1969, Bobby Hull received a special award, the Lester Patrick Trophy, presented to Bobby for his outstanding service to hockey.

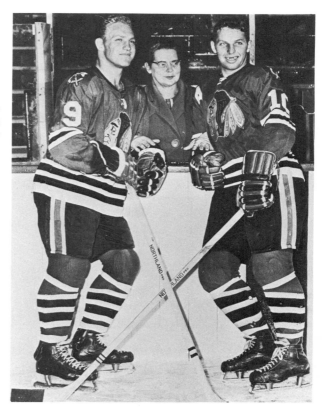

Teammates and brothers, Bobby and Dennis Hull, get a smile of approval from their proud mother.

Then he picked one of the hats off the ice and comically put it on his head while, smiling, he skated around the ice to acknowledge the cheers of the crowd.

In the remaining few games of the season, Bobby scored three more goals — to set the new record at fifty-four.

Bobby Hull scored fifty-two goals the next year, just to show that his record-breaking performance the year before had been no fluke. A couple of years later he broke his own record, with fifty-eight.

Bobby looks over his new contract with the WHA Winnipeg Jets.

By the time he left the National Hockey League after the 1972 season, Hull was second only to Gordie Howe among the all-time scorers. Howe had 786 goals in twenty-five seasons, Hull 604 in fifteen seasons.

Why did Bobby Hull quit the NHL after fifteen great seasons to go to the newly formed Winnipeg Jets of the World Hockey Association?

Some people offer one word — money. That is part of the answer, but not all. After all, he was making more than $100,00 a year in Chicago. To know the rest of the answer, you have to think back to the little boy in Point Anne, one of a family of eleven children.

You have to think back to the year he left home, at age thirteen, to go away and play hockey because his father — a hard-working man with a large family to support — thought Bobby's big chance in life was as a hockey player.

You have to think back, too, to how he set great aims for himself — and achieved them. Bobby won the scoring championship at twenty-one. He was the perennial all-star at left wing and he kept winning NHL individual trophies. He won the Hart Trophy, for being the most valuable player to his team. He was awarded the Lady Byng Memorial Trophy, for combining the highest level of gentlemanly conduct with excellent play.

One of pro hockey's most honored players, superstar Bobby Hull, proudly displays the Art Ross and Hart trophies presented to him in 1967.

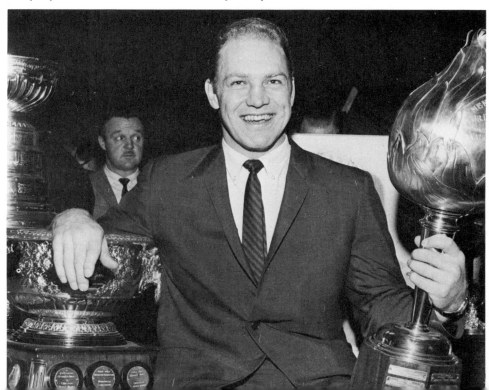

But all this time, off the ice, there was another Bobby Hull behind the star known to the fans.

There was a clue to this other Bobby in the way he would stand for an hour and sign autographs as long as there was anyone left who wanted one.

This different Bobby Hull went back to his own boyhood, skating the days away a few yards from home. He wanted something like that for his own boys. And he didn't feel they could get it in Chicago.

When the World Hockey Association was formed, the owners of the new clubs were aware that their success might depend on luring some great NHL stars to their teams. The greatest was Bobby Hull.

Winnipeg offered him a contract of nearly three million dollars over ten years. He signed with Winnipeg as a playing coach. It was the biggest sports story of the year.

The Hull home in Winnipeg has sixteen rooms. It has an indoor swimming pool. The family has grown to five children — four boys and a girl. There is lots of ice nearby for them to skate on.

And thirty miles east of Winnipeg, an easy drive, Bobby bought 700 acres and installed a big herd of beef cattle. No longer is it a matter of travelling hundreds of miles to his Ontario farm from wherever he happens to be playing. When the Winnipeg team is home, he can be at his farm in a matter of minutes.

Bobby and his wife, Joanne, happily greet the latest addition to their family — their first daughter.

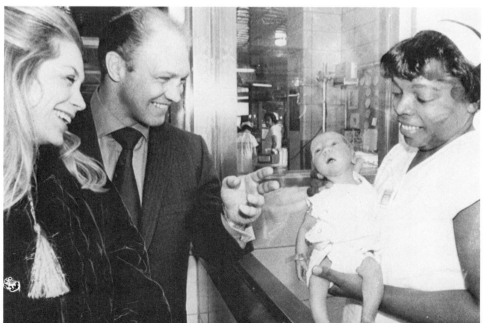

In the summer he builds fences, hand-feeds new born calves, runs his farm as a business operation, and loves it.

Also, all year long Bobby works hard to help the new league to be noticed and well thought-of. And he does it not only by scoring, although he scored fifty goals in his first year with the Jets.

This incident is typical. A little boy in a wheelchair was moving along a Winnipeg hospital corridor early one January when a big smiling man with clear blue eyes stopped beside him.

"Hello, son," said the stranger. "Do you like hockey?"

The wide-eyed little boy replied that he did.

"I'm glad to meet you," the visitor said. "I'm Bobby Hull. Have a happy new year." He put out his hand and the small boy eagerly put his tiny hand in the big one.

Bobby visits hospitals wherever he goes. He has a care for people who are not as fortunate as he has been in life. He never forgets how lucky he has been.

That is the special quality that Bobby Hull brings to his role as superstar. Once his wife said he was spending too much time away from home by going wherever there was a child who was sick or could use a lift.

Bobby could see her point. "But," he said, "maybe along the way I can help just one boy."

That is the special Bobby Hull, the superstar who never forgets what it is to be small and lonely, away from home, and not sure of what the future might bring.

ACKNOWLEDGMENTS

PHOTO CREDITS

Canada Wide Feature Service, Ltd., 8, 19, 22, 29, 31, 35; The Globe and Mail, Toronto, Canada, 36; Photograph by Robert Shaver, 13, 17, 28, 30; Toronto Sun Photo, 26, 33, 34, 38; United Press International, 10, 11, 14, 24, 27, 32, 37, 39; Wide World Photos, cover, 6, 7, 15, 20, 21, 25; Courtesy of Harvey Wineberg, (photo by Herb Nott and Co., Ltd., Toronto), 5; Courtesy of Harvey Wineberg, (photo by Focus Studio, Toronto), 18.